IT'S TRUE!

THE VIKINGS GOT LOST

Did you know that frogs are cannibals, fashion can be fatal and the dinosaurs never died? Or that redheads were once burned at the stake as witches? Find out why rubbish tips are like lasagna, and how maggots help solve crimes!

Books to make your brain bulge! Find out all about them on www.itstrue.com.au

DAVID GREAGG
PICTURES BY BINNY HOBBS

ALLEN&UNWIN

First published in 2006

Allen & Unwin
83 Alexander Street
Crows Nest NSW 2065
Australia
Phone: (61 2) 8425 0100
Fax: (61 2) 9906 2218
Email: info@allenandunwin.com
Web: www.allenandunwin.com

National Library of Australia
Cataloguing-in-Publication entry:

Greagg, David.
It's true! the vikings got lost.
Bibliography.
Includes index.
For children.
ISBN 1 74114 860 X.
1. Vikings – Juvenile literature. 2. Civilization, Viking – Juvenile literature. I. Hobbs, Binny.
II. Title. (Series : It's true! ; 19)
948.022

Series, cover and text design by Ruth Grüner
Cover photograph: Jomsvikings (www.jomsvikings.com)
Set in 12.5pt Minion by Ruth Grüner
Printed by McPherson's Printing Group

1 3 5 7 9 10 8 6 4 2

Teaching notes for the It's True! series are available on the website: www.itstrue.com.au

CONTENTS

WHY VIKINGS?

When I was a kid, my brother used to get a comic which had a serial in it called 'Karl The Viking'. It came out every month and we couldn't wait for the next episode. Everyone else around him panicked, but Karl stayed calm no matter what. He was cool.

Later, I learned the Viking language (Old Norse) and read the stories about Viking kings, heroes and explorers – men like Harald the Ruthless, Erik the Red. I found out that the Vikings discovered America way before Columbus. There were other surprises too. I learned that they almost invented pizza (the only thing missing was tomato), that horned helmets were definitely a no-no, and that a bunch of Vikings dressed in black spelt real trouble.

All in all, the Vikings were great fighters and great storytellers. I still think they are cool.

1

VIKINGS ON THE LOOSE

The Vikings lived in the far north of Europe 1500 years ago. Most of them were fair-haired, blue-eyed and very tall.[1] They probably shivered a lot. Winters in places close to the North Pole are generally long, dark, snowy, icy, windy and . . . well, wintry.

In between the winters were very short summers of endless daylight. You could sunbake almost 24/7

[1] The founder of Viking Normandy was so huge he was called Hrolf the Walker, because 'they could find no horse big enough for him to ride.'

if you wanted to. The downside is that not much grows when the warm season is so short, especially if the soil's no good. And the Vikings had some of the worst farmland in the world. Here's how it went:

bad soil + not much sun = not much food

Sounds like a recipe for hungry times. But they had one good thing – some of the best iron in the world. They also knew a lot about building boats. Solution? Make yourself some iron (or steel) swords, hop on a boat and go steal somebody else's stuff. In other words, go Viking!

The Vikings being rude

'Viking' comes from the word *vik*, meaning a bay or inlet.[2] 'Going viking' meant taking your ships from your own bays, putting them into other people's, and seeing what you could get. Waving a big iron sword around often helped persuade people to give you the things you wanted – gold, silver, furs, food and slaves. (There's a special word for this kind of robbery with violence: 'pillaging'.) If people offered you money to go away and annoy someone else, you took the money and left. But that wouldn't stop you coming back next year, to raid, loot, riot, pillage and cause mayhem.

[2] The name of Iceland's capital Reykjavik (Ray-kya-vik) means 'smoky bay'.

The Vikings were fierce and fearless warriors and would kill to get what they wanted. To other people they were very frightening – psycho nutcases, in fact.

The author of the *Anglo-Saxon Chronicle* (it sounds like a newspaper, but it was actually a monk's diary) wrote this:

'In this year [793 CE] there were exceptional flashes of lightning, and fiery dragons were seen flying in the air. A great famine soon followed these signs, and on the 8th of June in the same year the harrying of the heathen [Vikings] miserably destroyed God's church in Lindisfarne by rapine and slaughter.'

Dragons, famine and Viking warriors – it must have seemed as though all the demons of hell had been let loose.

For the next couple of centuries the Vikings (also called Norsemen) rampaged all over the known world. They terrorised most of the British Isles and northern France, and it seemed nothing and nobody could stop them. Only the little kingdom of Wessex (in what is now England) fought them off.

STRANGERS WHITE OR BLACK

The Irish called them **Finn-galls** (white strangers), **Dubh-galls** (black strangers) or **Lochlainn** (lakemen). They probably called them a lot of other things as well.

An Irish poet wrote on a cold winter's night:

Bitter is the wind tonight
tossing the sea's white hair.
This night I do not fear
the fierce warriors of Lochlainn.

Meaning that he did fear the Vikings, but he thought even they wouldn't be so crazy as to go out raiding in a wild storm.

The Vikings being polite

Where they could, the 'white strangers' made money by trading. This meant they had to remember their manners. Instead of saying 'Gimme that gold, or else!' they'd be saying, 'Look at this pure amber necklace! Be the envy of all the women in town! And remember, at Crazy Olaf's, we will *not* be beaten on price! One for you, sir? Thank you and have a good day.'

They sold:

furs
ivory
amber
jewellery
clothes
whalebone
rope
baby duck feathers
slaves

and they bought:

food

wood

gold and silver

other metals

slaves[3]

Their ships went absolutely everywhere in Europe and beyond, even as far as Africa. They made far more wealth by buying and selling stuff than they ever did by robbing people. It was easier too, because you didn't have to run away afterwards.

Why don't we hear about Viking traders? Well, trading wasn't really news in those days. The *Anglo-Saxon Chronicle* didn't have a Business section. Not many poets got excited about it either. So the Vikings' success in trade didn't make it into the history books of the time.

Put it this way: all we ever get to hear about is the raid and invade, not the trade.

[3] Anyone could become a slave if they were captured in battle. It wasn't as bad as it sounds. Slaves in those days weren't always kept in chains or beaten up all the time.

ON THE MOVE

The Vikings began life in southern Sweden (or Svithjoth as they called it) but began to move through the lands we now call Denmark and Norway around 400 CE. They terrorised and settled in large parts of England and Ireland between 800 and 1000 CE. They went even further afield to trade, along rivers right across Russia and by sea as far as Africa.

How Far Vikings traded

Where Vikings invaded and settled

Note: The map shows modern country names in English. These are not the names used by the Vikings.

Vikings came to stay

Some Norsemen decided to stay in the lands they travelled to. It makes sense. England and Ireland had far better soil and more sunshine for a start. English placenames from these times include Viking words. For example, Kirkby and Grimsby and York are Viking names (for example, York was Jorvik).

Ulf, Olaf and the Werewolf: Viking names

In the so-called Dark Ages (roughly 400 to 1100 CE), people didn't have family names the way Westerners do now (David Field, Janet Smith). So how did they know which David or Janet was which?

In the Highlands of Scotland you would just add the person's hair colour – you'd be Eachan Ruadh (Hector the Red-Haired) or Mairi Ban (Mary the Blonde). But in bigger communities this wouldn't be enough. The simplest way of telling people apart was to say whose son or daughter you were (Ian Johnson,

Maire Ni Dhiarmada – Mary daughter of Dermot).

Modern Iceland still doesn't have surnames – family names that are passed down to children and grandchildren. Icelandic phonebooks are arranged by first names. If you want to find David Oddson you just look in the book among all the Davids and keep going until you find Oddson. His son Bjorn would be under the Bs – Bjorn Davidson. Or, if you want Vigdis Finnbogadottir, you look up Vigdis and keep going till you find her. (She was Iceland's first woman President.)

One of the most famous of all Vikings was Egil (pronounced 'Ail') Skallagrimsson. His father was called Skallagrim. Egil's grandfather was simply called Kveldulf (Evening-Wolf), because he apparently turned into a werewolf when the sun set. Not the sort of guy you'd want to mess with.

If you didn't want to be known as Someone's Son, what happened? Well, many Vikings we know of had second names given to them by friends and family, and a pretty strange lot they are. Here are some famous Viking names:

Mord Fiddle
Ulf the Unwashed
Bjorn Butter-Box
Sigurd Snake-Eye
Thorolf Creek-Nose
Domnal Seal's-Head
Ketil Flatnose
Olaf Peacock
Hrolf Bean-Pole
Ragnar Hairy-Pants
Gunnlaug Snake-Tongue
Eystein Fart
Einar Stomach-Shaker
Brynjolf Camel

As you can see, they had a slightly odd sense of humour.

AND THEN THERE WAS HROLF

A farm boy called Vogg went to see King Hrolf at his court. The boy walked round and round the throne until Hrolf asked what he was doing.

'I came here to see the great King Hrolf,' said Vogg, 'but all I find is this long bean-pole of a man.'

King Hrolf laughed. 'A gift should go with a naming; but you have nothing suitable to give me. So I'd better give you a gift instead.' He took out a beautiful sword and gave it to Vogg.

'Thank you, Sire,' said Vogg. 'And if anyone ever kills you, I will avenge you with this sword.'

And that's why King Hrolf was known as Hrolf Bean-Pole.

It seems rather strange to say 'I will avenge you' rather than 'I will protect you from dying,' but that was a very Viking attitude. If you were fated to die, that was that. But you could protest against Fate by sticking something pointy into your lord's killer.

Hrolf Bean-Pole

2

VIKINGS AT HOME

As well as being traders and travellers, raiders and looters, the Vikings were fishers and farmers. They lived simply. Viking houses were usually made of wood. (In Iceland and Greenland trees were rare and wood was precious, so people used stone and earth for house-building there. Some families had grass growing on their roofs!) If you were rich, you might have several rooms, but many families lived in just one big room with a fire in the middle.

If you were a man, you'd spend a lot of time farming. You'd also hunt animals, seals, walrus and

birds, or go fishing. If you were a woman, you'd spin or weave cloth and sew it into clothes. You'd churn butter, and make cheese and yogurt and bread. When you weren't out fishing, hunting, farming, playing or pillaging, you'd cook, eat or play games around the fire. You'd make or repair tools, nets, weapons, jewellery. The Vikings were skilled wood-workers, weavers, metal-workers and bone-carvers.

In the evenings, people would light the fish-oil lamps and tell stories and recite poems. Outside, the wind would be howling around the roof, but inside you would be warm and well-fed, with the fire casting dancing shadows on the

walls. The fish-oil lamps gave a strong yellow light – and (naturally) a strong fishy smell. The people weren't too bad, though. Vikings washed in hot baths once a week, and they were fresher-smelling than most modern Europeans. One Saxon writer complained that all the local girls preferred Viking men to their own. They smelt nicer.

Later on, the lamps would be put out and you'd go to sleep in your straw bed. This wasn't too prickly, because animal skins stopped the straw from sticking into your face. In the morning (if you were smart enough to stay in bed while Mum built up the fire) you would smell barley-cakes cooking.

Time to get dressed? If you're a boy, you slept in a knee-length linen shirt. Now you add a pair of long woollen trousers held up with string, and a woollen tunic, also knee-length. Then you put on socks and shoes, and if you're going out into the cold, pin a heavy woollen cloak on your right shoulder. If you're a girl, you put on a long linen dress and then a woollen wrap-around apron, held up by two large decorative brooches.

DUCK FOR COVER

For really cold weather, Vikings wore clothes padded with down (baby feathers) gathered from wild ducks. Down is very warm, far warmer than normal feathers.

Vikings were fierce in battle, but they were very gentle with their baby ducks. They made little nesting-places for the ducks to lay eggs in. They waited till the ducks had finished with the nests, then gathered the feathers and sewed them between layers of cloth as padding.

Men in black

Vikings used plant dyes to make different colours for their clothes. There was only one colour to worry about. If you saw a bunch of guys dressed in black coming towards you, it was time to run away and stay away until the excitement was over. To the Vikings, black was the colour of revenge. Someone been killed in your family? No settlement arranged? Get a few friends together, dress up in black and go calling. It was actually a good way of telling everyone else to clear out of harm's way.

Horned helmets? No thanks

Did the Vikings ever wear horned helmets? The short answer is 'No', even if most pictures show them that way. Why would you? It's a stupid idea and the Vikings weren't stupid. You might as well put a sticker on your hat saying, 'Grab this bit here to make it *really*

easy to kill me.' So why does everyone think they had horns? A nineteenth-century artist called Malmstrom got a bit carried away when he was illustrating Frithjof's Saga. The story was incredibly boring and stupid, and Malmstrom decided to spice it up with something really outlandish. So in went the horned helmets.

Fish and no chips

What did the Vikings eat? Everything they could get their hands on. Fish, butter, cheese, bread, yogurt, plus in summer berries, fruit, vegies, eggs – and meat when they could get it. They'd eat anything that moved, flapped, waddled, swam or tried to run away – red deer, cattle, sheep, goats, pigs, chickens, geese, ducks and many other sorts of birds. They dried or salted meat to put away for the long, hungry winter. ('Anyone want a piece of dried walrus?') Of course they liked fish. You name it, they ate it, from whale steaks to sardines. And yes, they ate dried fish in winter – yum, dried fish. But sadly, they had no chips. Potatoes were unknown in Europe before the 1600s.

THE VIKINGS ATE PIZZA!

We said that Vikings ate bread. They also made a kind of pizza, believe it or not. This was mostly in Denmark and other countries further south. In the freezing north, growing wheat or barley for flour wasn't really possible.

INGREDIENTS

Base: 7 cups wheat flour,
3 cups buttermilk, 1 egg, pinch salt

Topping: chopped meat and cheese OR fruit, nuts, honey OR toasted stinging nettles (true!)* OR fish and shellfish

Mix flour, buttermilk, egg and salt, and knead. Shape into small balls and flatten on a sheet of metal. Press topping into each one and cook in a hot oven for about 10 minutes. Tap it and if it sounds hollow, it's ready.

* Toasted stinging nettle sounds a lot worse than it is. It's not too different from spinach or other greens on a modern pizza. Of course, if you put *raw* nettles on your pizza they will bite you back . . .

Viking board games

The Vikings loved board games. They called these games *tafl* (tables). Unlike our chess or draughts, they often had unequal sides. In *Hnefatafl*, the board can be anything from 7 x 7 up to 19 x 19 squares, and Black will only have half the number of pieces that White does. For a big board, Black will have 12 pieces and White 24.

The pieces move in straight lines like a castle in chess, and you can take a piece if you trap it between two of your own. The idea of the game is for Black (who moves first) to get his king into one of the corner squares. White tries to trap the king with his pieces so the king can't move.

The Saxons (who lived in Germany and later England) also played *Hnefatafl*. They called it King-Stone, which is a lot easier to remember and pronounce.

Vikings knew how to play chess – they'd picked it up in the Middle East. Their name for it was *Shaktafl*. Maybe chess helped pass the time on those lo-o-ong winter evenings.

The Vikings also played dice games. The dice might

have different numbers on them (one set has the numbers 3, 4, 4, 5, 5 and 6). Sometimes they weren't cubes. Many Viking dice are like long square-ended rods, with the numbers 1 and 2 on the ends. One board game (*Kvatrutafl*) used these long dice to make the game more complicated. Dice were made from antlers, bone, walrus tusks, jet (a black stone), wood or horn.

Did the Vikings cheat? It looks as though some of them did. People have found Viking dice loaded with small weights inside.

3

ACROSS THE WORLD WITHOUT A COMPASS

Viking longships were incredibly well built. They were light, fast, flexible, easy to steer, and didn't need great depth of water beneath them. You could run a Viking ship into the mouth of a river and sail it upstream without going aground. This meant that you could land your army anywhere near a river, come ashore, pass the time of day with the locals, set fire to everything and disappear again.

HOW TO BUILD A VIKING LONGSHIP

(1) First, choose your tree. It should be a big tree without many knots in the wood – an oak tree. You don't want your ship to fall apart in mid-pillage, and oak is very tough. (Oak was also sacred to Othin, god of war.)

For the planks and ribs, use whatever you can get – ash, elm, pine or larch. But the keel, bow and stern will always be made from oak.

(2) Cut down your tree with axes and small wooden wedges. Why not use a saw? Simple: saws were incredibly expensive and you use them only for the fiddly bits.

(3) You should leave half of the tree in one piece, to be used for the keel. Split the rest into planks with mallets and more wedges and plane them down with adzes and maybe a spokeshave (a sort of two-handed chisel).

(4) When the long planks are ready, you'll need to bend them into shape.

(5) The planks fit over each other so you get overlapping plates of wood, which you will fit by hand into the keel and fasten there with small pegs or rivets.

The overlapping planks of wood make the ship flexible. It will bend a little when sailing through waves, which gives a smoother ride.

(6) Put in wooden ribs across the ship. Then fix the mast, the bow and the stern (front and back) into the keel.

(7) Your bowpiece will probably be carved into the shape of a dragon's head. Just the thing your enemies would want to see nosing up their river . . .

(8) Add rigging, water-barrels, a big square sail and a steering oar, and hey presto! you have your longship.

The ship-building process has taken you months and was hugely expensive. But you're a Viking and you fully intend to get your money back, and more . . .

Wandering in the rain

There were two drawbacks to Viking ships. One was that they got rather wet in a storm. They had animal-skin tarpaulins that you could stretch over the decking. But it must have been like having a shower in your clothes when it rained.

The other problem was that they didn't have compasses to help them find their way. Instead they had a wooden bowl with a small stick on top. You held it up to the midday sun and the shadow showed you where north was – like a sundial. But . . . you can see the problem. They only knew where they were going while the sun kept shining. If a fog came down, they got lost.

As for night navigation, forget it. They did know how to steer by the stars, but there was a catch. Most of the time, the only stars you see in northern seas are when you get hit on the head by the mast.

'Hey Dad, where are you?'

Bjarni Herjolfson got lost in the year 986 CE. He was on his way from Norway to visit his father in Greenland, and the fog came down for three days. So he and his crew sailed on blind, wondering where they were. They sighted land. 'Is this Greenland?' the crew wanted to know. 'No, Greenland is mountainous and covered in glaciers,' said Bjarni. 'This is flat and covered in small flat rocks.' (Later, Leif Eriksson decided to call this island Small-Flat-Rock-Land.)[4]

[4] Leif was good at exploring, but absolutely terrible at names. We think this was Baffin Island in northern Canada.

They sailed north and found another land which had a glacier on it. Bjarni thought this land was absolutely good for nothing, so he kept looking for Greenland, which he found eventually. When he got home, Bjarni told everyone about the new lands he'd discovered. 'Why didn't you have a look around?' everyone wanted to know. Bjarni said, 'All I wanted to do was get to Greenland to see Dad – get lost!' Which was odd, as he was the one who'd got lost.

Next stop: Iceland

Bjarni wasn't the first Viking to lose his way sailing west. In 860 CE Gartharr Svavarsson was sailing around Denmark and got caught up in a terrific storm. Eventually he found Iceland. Iceland is over 1000 kilometres from Denmark, so he was definitely off course! When he got home, he told everyone about it. 'It's got volcanoes and glaciers next to each other, so you can have a spa bath any time you like,' he said. Many Vikings thought this sounded pretty good, so they decided to settle there.

The red and the green?

One Viking who didn't get lost was Erik the Red. He had managed to get himself exiled from Norway for killing some people, so he settled in Iceland. Different country, same result – he started arguing with people and saying it with battle-axes. 'Out!' said the Icelanders. So he decided to emigrate to Greenland, and took 25 ships with him. Only 14 got there.

Erik the Red's bunch of Vikings stayed in Greenland for over 300 years, though you really have to wonder why. Greenland is pretty much covered with ice all year round. (By contrast, Iceland is mostly green. The Vikings were a bit odd about names, you have to admit.)

Who gave it the name Greenland? None other than Erik the Red himself. He said that if the new land had a good name, then men of worth would want to settle there. Strange but true. You could call Erik the pin-up boy of real-estate agents. It was his son, Leif Eriksson, who gave the name Small-Flat-Rock-Land to the island Bjarni bumped into by mistake.

Finding the big one

Leif Eriksson should be famous. He was the first Viking to settle in America, hundreds of years before Christopher Columbus. He lived in a cold, snowy part of North America that we now call Newfoundland. A proper Viking house was recently dug up in Newfoundland, so they really did stay there. The locals were anything but friendly, so after a few years Leif and his friends went home again.

Leif called the new country Vinland, and some people think it means that he found grapes there (Vinland = Wine-land). But the word *vinn* also means pasture, so Vinland = Grass-land seems a whole lot more likely.

4

LAND OF FIRE AND ICE

By the late ninth century (the 800s), Sweden and Denmark were ruled by one king each. Norway was a collection of tiny little kingdoms. Or it was until King Harald came along.

One of Norway's kingdoms was called Westfold, and its young King Harald sent word to a beautiful girl called Gytha that she was to be his new girlfriend. (He already had several.) 'Oh yeah?' said Gytha. 'If you were king of all Norway, then I'd think about it.' Well, goodness, thought Harald, what do I do now? Should I carry her off by force? Maybe not – my grandfather

Guthroth married Queen Asa by force, and she had him killed. Anyway, abducting women really isn't what Vikings do. Hmmm . . .

Harald was a determined man. He proclaimed that he would neither cut nor comb his hair until he was king of all Norway. After a few years he had conquered all his enemies, probably with the help of his by now extremely smelly hairdo. He was called Harald Mop-Hair, though not when he was listening.

Then he had the Viking equivalent of a haircut, shampoo and blow-dry, and all of a sudden his hair was so beautiful that he became known as Harald Fine-Hair. 'OK, are you impressed now?'

he asked Gytha. 'That will do nicely,' she said, and joined the royal household.

No to Norway, yes to Iceland

Many powerful Vikings in Norway weren't at all impressed. 'We've never had a king of all Norway before and we don't want one now,' they said. Defeated by King Harald in battle, some decided to go and live in Iceland instead, alongside the volcanoes and the glaciers.

Nobody was living there. When the first Norwegian settlers arrived, they found some huts in the Vestmannaeyjar Islands where some Irish monks had gone to get away from it all. But the monks had been dead for centuries.

The first settler was Ingolf Arnarson, who set out from Norway with his friends, family, sheep, cattle, tools, kitchen goods and the worst case of sea-sickness in history. While still at sea, he threw his sacred doorposts overboard and promised to settle wherever they came ashore. He didn't find them at first, so he settled somewhere else. Three years later he found the doorposts at the place we now call Reykjavik and made his home there. Soon many of the toughest and bravest Vikings followed him. (Not everyone was impressed, though. 'That place of fish will never see me in my old age,' Ketil Flat-Nose told his sons in disgust. He went to Scotland instead.)

Things but no kings

'No more kings,' said the settlers. They divided Iceland up into 39 districts, each with its own chieftain. Lawsuits would be judged at district gatherings (or Things, as they were called). Once a year everyone would go to a place called Thingvellir (Assembly Plain) for the Althing, the really big gathering and law court.

When you got to the Althing, you had to be prepared to do a lot of listening. Each year the Law-Speaker, who was appointed for three years, would have to recite one-third of the laws of Iceland from memory.

The Althing was a kind of fair, agricultural show, High Court and (sometimes) battlefield all in one. Rich people and traders had booths. The walls stood all year round, and every year you just put a new roof on to make a temporary house or shop for the summer.

People bought and sold woollen clothes, furs, woodwork, butter, cheese, fish and meat. Children played a bat and ball game, while grown-ups gossiped and argued.

Most importantly, people came to the Althing to get judgement on their lawsuits. There is a story about a merchant called Ale-Hood, who accidentally burnt down his own forest. And another forest belonging to six other chieftains. At the Althing everyone agreed that Ale-Hood was a pathetic creature, but as it was an accident he shouldn't be punished too severely. So the heavies said that Ale-Hood only had to pay a small fine and the six chieftains could accept it or else (meaning accept it or they'd get a battle-axe in their heads by return of post).

There was no police force or army. If you wanted your case heard, you needed to get some powerful chieftain to help you out in pleading your case. Fights broke out from time to time, but were eventually settled by payments of silver to the injured (or more injured) parties.

MURDER OR JUST MAYHEM?

The Vikings didn't think of killing the way we do. They accepted it as long as it was done by the rules. If you cut Thrain's head off during a discussion about something or other, you'd go to the nearest house and knock on the door. You would say, 'Thrain is dead, I am responsible for the killing, I have covered the body and I'll see his relatives at the Assembly.'

If Thrain had been particularly annoying, his family would probably say 'OK, 200 ounces of silver, thanks, and we'll say no more about it.' If Thrain had just been minding his own business, you would most likely be outlawed and have to leave the country. Or the family might get a homeboy posse together and pay you a visit. With battle-axes. And this (the posse) was all perfectly legal, because nobody had to accept a settlement if they didn't feel like it. Then *your* relatives would have to come to an agreement with the people who had killed *you*. It was a bit weird, but it worked pretty well.

Takeover

Iceland kept its independence until the thirteenth century (the 1200s). Eventually, the kings of Norway decided that Iceland belonged to them. One of the people who tried to keep Iceland independent was Snorri Sturlusson. He was Law-Speaker twice, and wrote a history of the kings of Norway and several sagas (Viking novels) while sitting in a hot tub. Snorri told the kings of Norway that he'd mind Iceland for them, but unfortunately they didn't listen and took over anyway. Iceland didn't become free again until 1918.

5

BEDTIME STORIES

The Vikings' idea of a good bedtime story had nothing to do with ducks and rabbits and Harry the Dirty Dog. They didn't go for that stuff. They liked a juicy war story, or a thriller with a few axe-murders thrown in – a bit of a bloodbath.

These bedtime stories were called Sagas. The word just means 'long story', and each district had its own family saga. The ones we know about were written by Icelandic authors. Most of the action takes place in Iceland, but the heroes usually go abroad at some point and impress the kings of Norway, Sweden and

Denmark. The idea was that if you were a real hero, you had to make it among the big boys.

The sagas aren't exactly history. They were more like ve-e-ery long bedtime stories about grandparents, great-grandparents and way-back ancestors. Listening to a story around the fire was a good way of spending long, cold, dark winter evenings. There were a lot of these evenings to get through. After all, winter in Iceland lasts about eight months!

The three most famous sagas are Njal's Saga, Laxdaela Saga and Egil's Saga.

Axing for trouble: Evil Egil

Egil's Saga describes the life of Egil Skallagrimsson: poet, sorcerer and axe-murderer. (He was the one whose grandfather was a werewolf.)

Even as a child, Egil was cranky and bad-tempered. When he was 12, he was playing a ball game (probably something like Irish hurling) and doing badly, so he tried to hit his opponent with the bat. The other children took the bat from him and threw him to the ground. Most kids would run away and cry at this point. Not Egil. He ran away all right, but came back with a battle-axe and killed his opponent. After that his parents began to think that he would be better off going Viking and finding other people to annoy.

Later, he got in trouble with King Erik Blood-Axe of Norway and his scary wife Queen Gunnhild. He decided to leave Norway, but before he left he planted a Nithstong, or stake of scorn, on the sea-coast. It was a long staff with runes carved on it and a horse's head on the top. The runes were Egil's spell to bring bad stuff down upon the King and Queen, and they worked – sort of. Later, Egil was shipwrecked near York in England and found that Erik and Gunnhild weren't King and Queen of Norway any more. They were now King and Queen of York. Oops.

Egil realised they wouldn't be too pleased to see him, but he went to the court anyway. Erik Blood-Axe said he'd let Egil go if he came up with a poem in praise of Good King Erik by morning. Gunnhild was all in favour of cutting off his head then and there (I said she was scary). She cast spells until midnight to try to put Egil off, but by morning Egil had finished his poem. He recited it to the King, who let him go to Iceland.

In Iceland, Egil killed quite a few people. You would think by now that someone would have killed *him*. Instead, he grew to be terribly old and blind, and died in his bed. Long afterwards, somebody dug up his body and tried to smash his skull with a battle-axe. The skull turned white, but it wasn't even chipped.

Perhaps people *had* tried to get rid of Egil and found he was axe-proof?[5]

Burnt Njal

In **Njal's Saga**, there are two main heroes. Gunnar is the best fighter in Iceland, but he prefers not to fight at all unless he has to. Njal is no fighter, but he is praised even more than Gunnar as a famous lawyer and peace-maker. Their enemies (and even their wives) try to stir up trouble between them, but Gunnar and Njal say, 'We will never fight each other, so you may as well stop trying.'

The only problem is that there are more than enough people trying to cause trouble elsewhere, and eventually the two heroes are drawn into it. Njal tells Gunnar never to kill more than once in the same family, but Gunnar does. He is outlawed, and prepares

[5] It sounds as though Egil was an out-and-out murderer who actually enjoyed killing. He probably was. Experts say that the hardness of his skull proves he had a brain disease which made him very violent.

to leave Iceland. A posse turns up at his house to kill him.

Gunnar is shooting arrows from the windows. The bowstring breaks, so he asks his beautiful wife Hallgerth for two locks of her hair. 'Does anything depend on this?' she asks him. 'My life,' he tells her.

'In that case I remember a slap you once gave me,' says Hallgerth (meaning she won't help him).

'Everyone has to earn fame their own way,' Gunnar says. 'You won't be asked again.'

Gunnar kills two of the posse and wounds eight more before they kill him. 'Can we have ground to bury our dead?' asks Gizur the White, the leader.

'Gladly,' says Gunnar's mother. 'But I would rather

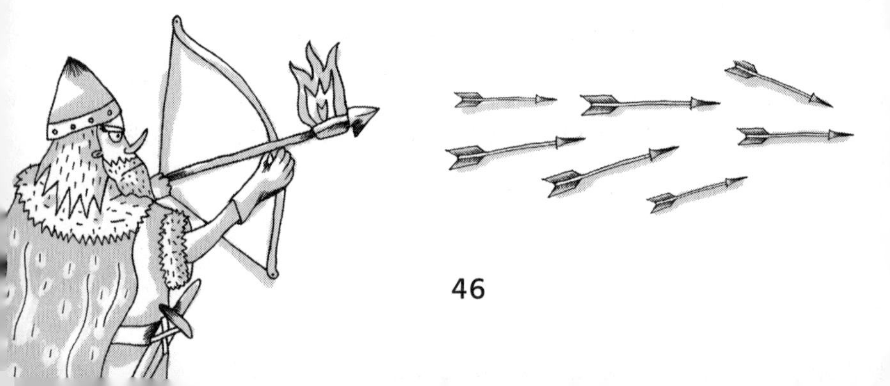

have given enough land to bury the lot of you.'

'You can't be blamed for saying that,' he tells her.

Later, Njal and his sons are drawn into more fighting. Njal tries to keep the peace but it becomes impossible, especially with Skarp-Hethin (his eldest son) on the rampage. At the Althing, Njal gathers a huge pile of silver to be given out to all the relatives of people his sons have killed. Skarp-Hethin insults Flosi, the opposing chieftain. There is nothing for it but war. In the end, Njal and his sons are burned in their house. His nephew Kari escapes, and chases Flosi's men around the world, killing them one by one.

Finally Kari and his friends are shipwrecked in a snowstorm off Svinafell. This is Flosi's country.

'Now we will see what sort of chieftain he is,' says Kari. He and his men walk straight into Flosi's hall. What does Flosi do? He stands up and throws his arms around Kari and invites him to sit in the high seat next to him. And they are friends from that day on.

The writer is telling us that to be a real Viking hero, you have to make peace with your enemies.

VIKING WOMEN

If you were a woman in the Middle Ages, it paid to be a Viking. Viking women had more power, and more say in their own lives, than women in other places.

hi boys!

If you were a Viking woman

- ★ You could own land.
- ★ You could usually choose your husband, and couldn't be married by force.
- ★ You could divorce your husband if you didn't like him or he behaved badly. In Laxdaela Saga Guthrun divorced her husband because he slapped her once.
- ★ When you got married, your father gave presents and money to your husband. This was called a dowry. If you got divorced, you got half of the dowry back.

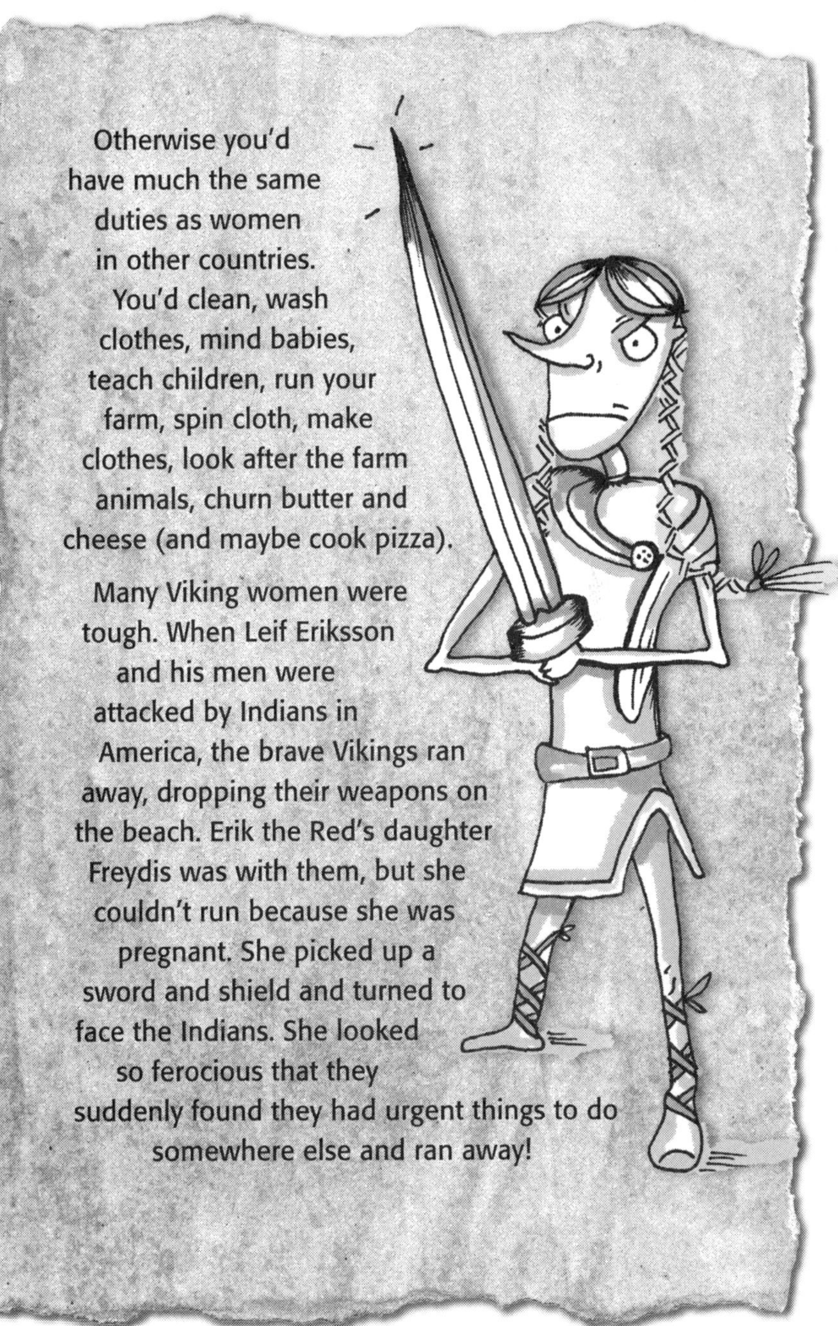

Otherwise you'd have much the same duties as women in other countries. You'd clean, wash clothes, mind babies, teach children, run your farm, spin cloth, make clothes, look after the farm animals, churn butter and cheese (and maybe cook pizza).

Many Viking women were tough. When Leif Eriksson and his men were attacked by Indians in America, the brave Vikings ran away, dropping their weapons on the beach. Erik the Red's daughter Freydis was with them, but she couldn't run because she was pregnant. She picked up a sword and shield and turned to face the Indians. She looked so ferocious that they suddenly found they had urgent things to do somewhere else and ran away!

The revenge of Queen Sigrith

Queen Sigrith is mentioned in Olaf's Saga. King Olaf Tryggvason wanted to marry her. She liked him, but pointed out that he was already married to someone else. He couldn't see any problem with two wives, so he gave her a wedding ring. She thought it looked a bit funny and broke it in half. Sure enough, it wasn't real gold at all, but copper. Finally he wanted to convert her to Christianity. When she wouldn't, he slapped her face and asked, 'Why should I marry you, you heathen dog?'

'This may well be your death,' she said, and left. Later she married his bitterest enemy, King Svein Forkbeard of Denmark. There was a terrible sea-battle, where Olaf's ship the *Long Serpent* (the biggest Viking ship ever built) went up against Svein's fleet. The Norwegians were defeated and King Olaf was drowned.

Rule One: never slap a Viking woman!

6

WHAT, NO FIGHTING?

One saga where nobody gets killed at all is **Authun's Story**. Authun was a man from western Iceland who went on a trip to Greenland and brought back a magnificent polar bear.

'What will you do with it?' everyone wanted to know.

'I'm going to give it to King Svein Forkbeard of Denmark,' he said.

'Are you crazy?' his friends asked him. 'How will you get there? You'll have to go through Norway, and Norway and Denmark are at war!'

'Maybe I'll be lucky,' said Authun.

When he landed in Norway, King Harald the Ruthless sent for him and asked if he had anything valuable. Authun said yes, he had a bear.

'Will you give it to me for the price you paid for it?'

'No, I don't wish that, Lord,' said Authun.

King Harald thought about it. 'OK, double what you paid.'

'No thank you, Lord,' said Authun.

'Well, will you give it to me?'

'No, Lord.'

'What are you going to do with it, then?' King Harald wanted to know.

'I was going to Denmark to give it to King Svein,' Authun answered.

'Are you completely bonkers?' asked Harald. 'Don't you know he and I are at war?'

'Well, it's up to you,' said Authun. 'But maybe things will turn out all right for me.'

King Harald was impressed by Authun's laid-back attitude. He forgot to be ruthless this time and let Authun go. 'One one condition,' he added. 'Come back and tell me how it all turned out.'

Authun promised he would do that, and sailed to Denmark. There's a whole lot more story about what happened there – the short version is that the Danish king was pleased with the bear and invited Authun to stay for a long time. Finally Authun said he must go home.

'Why?' asked King Svein. 'I'll be offended if you don't stay and be my cup-bearer.' (A cup-bearer brings the royal drinking-horn to the king at feasts – a high honour.)

Authun explained that he had left enough money to support his mother in Iceland for three years, and the time was nearly up. 'All right,' said the King. 'I can't think of any other reason that wouldn't have made me cross.' He gave Authun many presents and sent him home with a ship loaded with valuable cargo.

Authun stopped off in Norway and went to see King Harald again. 'OK,' said the King. 'Tell me, how did King Svein pay you for the bear?'

'First, he accepted the gift,' said Authun.

'Yes, I would have too. What then?'

'Then, he gave me a lot of money to go to Rome,' said Authun.

'Well, so would I. What else?'

'When I came back with nothing, he took me in again and offered to make me his cup-bearer,' said Authun.

'That was a great honour, and I would have done the same. What else?'

'Then he gave me a trading ship to bring to Norway,' said Authun.

'That was generous, too. Anything else?'

'He told me that even if I lost the ship, I would still have this bag of silver,' said Authun.

'That was really generous,' said King Harald. 'I would have thought I'd done enough by giving you the ship. Tell me, when did he stop repaying you?'

'Finally he gave me this arm-ring to show I had

given King Svein a royal gift,' answered Authun. 'But he also said that if I owed an obligation to a man of note, then I should give the arm-ring to him. You are that man, Lord, because you could have imprisoned me and taken my bear anyway.'

King Harald accepted the arm-ring, and gave Authun another ship filled with cargo to take home to Iceland. So Authun sailed home to meet his mum, a rich man. He was lucky, and shrewd, but the Vikings always admired lucky men. You didn't have to kill people to be a famous Viking.

The Viking and the dragon

In the **Saga of Hrolf Bean-Pole**, a man called Bjarki helps a young man to become a hero. The story starts when Bjarki stays the night in a peasant's house. His host asks him if he is going to take service with King Hrolf. Bjarki says yes. Apparently there is a dragon terrorising the capital and he means to do something about it.

'In that case, could you look out for my son Hott?' says the peasant. 'He has gone to court, but I don't think he's doing well there.'

When Bjarki gets to the King's court, he finds all the men throwing bones at Hott, who has built himself a fort with them. Bjarki catches one of the bones and throws it back so hard that the man is killed. Bjarki tips him off his seat and takes his place. Then he lifts Hott out of his fort and tells him, 'No more bone-forts for you.'

That night, Bjarki goes out with Hott and eventually sticks his sword into the dragon. Exit dragon. He feeds

the dragon's heart to Hott to make him strong and wrestles with him. Then he spends the rest of the night being a very busy Viking indeed.

Next morning, King Hrolf and his men go out to face the dragon, which still looks very menacing. 'Who will go and kill the dragon?' asks the King.

'Send Hott,' says Bjarki. 'Well, OK,' says the King. 'If you think so . . .'

So Hott goes over the hill and kills the dragon. It's more like a Chinese New Year's dragon than a fire-breathing monster because Bjarki has been propping it up with sticks and ropes to make it look fearsome. Hott kills it anyway. Everyone cheers.

'He didn't kill the dragon,' says King Hrolf to Bjarki. 'You did.'

'Well, there may be something in that,' says Bjarki modestly.

'All right,' says King Hrolf. He gives Hott a famous sword and tells him his name shall be Hjalti (Sword-Hilt) and he will be one of the King's chosen men. Probably King Hrolf thought that if Bjarki felt Hott was worth bothering with then he must be OK.

7

RUNES + ROCKS = GRAFFITI

The Vikings weren't much into writing. They said or sang their stories. At other times they liked to get out and about and start pillaging. But they did have a special alphabet of 16 letters, called runes, which you could carve into wood or rocks. Here is one version of Viking runes:

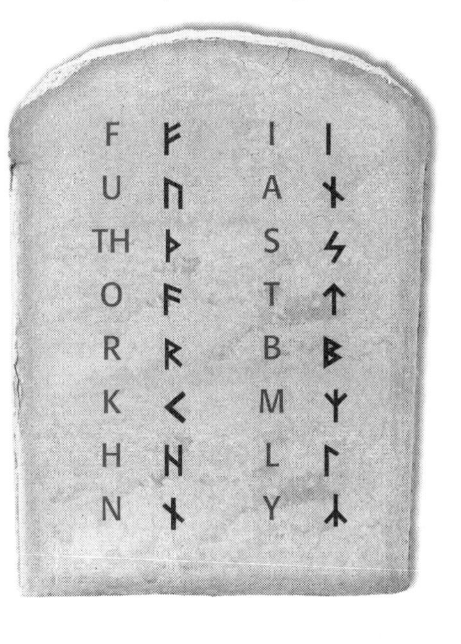

You will notice that there's no letter E. It's the most popular letter in English (check out the Scrabble board), but it wasn't nearly as common in Old Viking.

Just as our word 'alphabet' comes from the first two letters in Greek (and Hebrew), the runes are called 'futhork', from the first six letters of the runic alphabet.

What did the Vikings write with their runes? Short messages, for a start – it takes a while to carve letters in stone. Sometimes it really is just graffiti. The earliest runes we have are from about 400 CE in Norway. They're pretty basic: 'Dag made these runes.' A sword was found in a burial mound in Ireland with 'Domnal Seal's-Head owns this sword' scratched on it. (This meant but didn't say, 'So keep your thieving hands off it!')

THOR WAS HERE

Here's another, carved on a bone found in Norway:

'I loved her as a maiden, but I will not bother Erlend's horrible wife. It will be better when she is a widow.'

Some of the most intriguing Viking runes were found at Maes Howe in Orkney (off the northern tip of Scotland). They are mostly about women.

One piece says, 'Ingibjorg is the most beautiful of ladies.'

'Many a woman has walked stooping in here,' says another, signed by a man called Erlend.

The Vikings never lived in Maes Howe, but at least two Viking expeditions landed there, hoping to hide from enemies. The **Saga of the Orkney-Men** tells how Harald Maddadarson and his men camped there to escape a storm. During the night, the ghosts of dead kings threw things around the tomb and two of Harald's men went mad, and had to be carried around afterwards. It was, wrote the saga's author, 'rather inconvenient'.[6]

[6] The sagas were spoken stories to start with. It wasn't until the 1300s that the Icelandic ones were written down. Writers used vellum (animal skins) – they didn't have paper. They wrote with quill pens (sharpened feathers), dipped in ink made from hawthorn bark, wine and iron.

Some people think there's a treasure buried in Maes Howe. Ridiculous. The Vikings would never leave anything valuable, anywhere at all, if they could help it. Little things like ghosts or poltergeists wouldn't stand in their way.

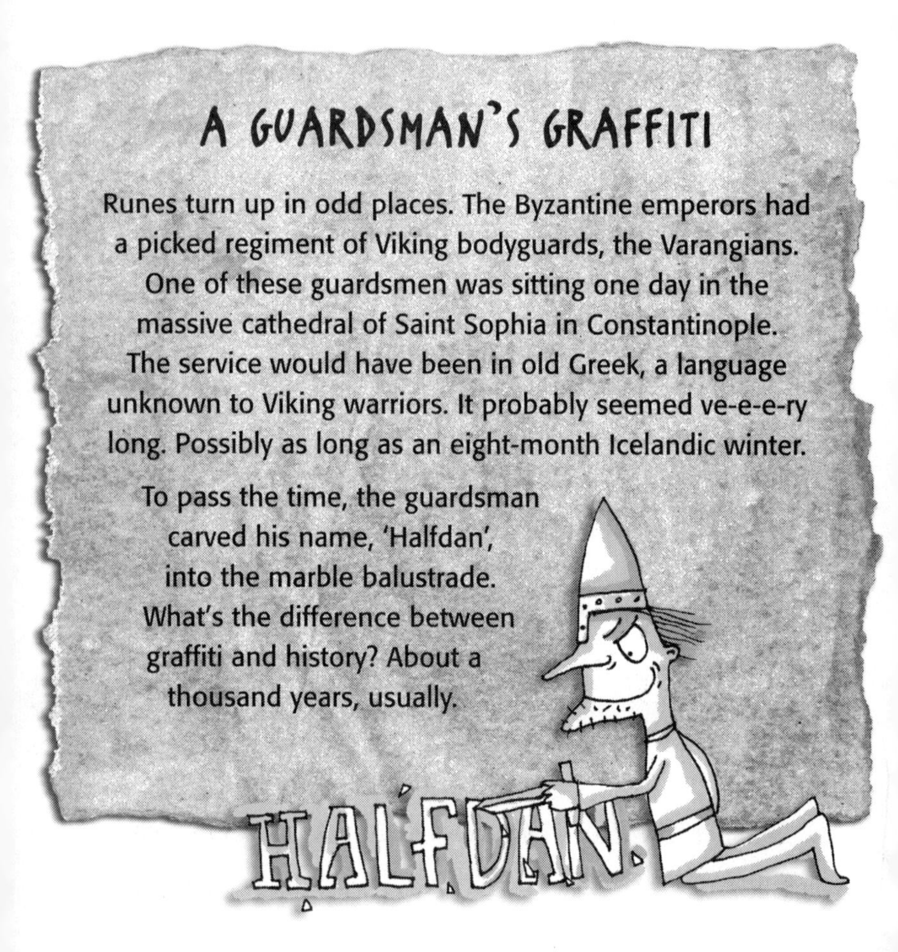

A GUARDSMAN'S GRAFFITI

Runes turn up in odd places. The Byzantine emperors had a picked regiment of Viking bodyguards, the Varangians. One of these guardsmen was sitting one day in the massive cathedral of Saint Sophia in Constantinople. The service would have been in old Greek, a language unknown to Viking warriors. It probably seemed ve-e-e-ry long. Possibly as long as an eight-month Icelandic winter.

To pass the time, the guardsman carved his name, 'Halfdan', into the marble balustrade. What's the difference between graffiti and history? About a thousand years, usually.

8

GODS AND THUNDER

Around the year 1000 CE, the Vikings converted to Christianity. Before that, they had their own gods, and terrifying they were too. Othin (or Odin) was the father of the gods. He had only one eye (he had given up the other to learn wisdom) and was followed around by two ravens called Hugin and Mugin

(Mind and Memory). He also had an eight-legged magic horse called Sleipnir. People believed that Othin liked human sacrifices, so at times whole armies might be killed to please him.

Othin was most revered in Sweden. The Norwegians and Icelanders usually preferred Thor, the god of thunder. Thor was also the god of farmers, and carried an enormous hammer called Mjollnir. He travelled around in a chariot drawn by two sacred goats, and was (for us) a much nicer god than Othin. Short-tempered, yes. A bit simple? Yes again. But at least he didn't expect human sacrifices.

Frey and Freya were god and goddess of the harvest, and also of love. Loki was the clown, but a very unpleasant clown who liked crude practical jokes. You didn't mess with him. There were many others. They all lived in a place called Valholl, or Hall of the Slain, in the city of Asgarth. Vikings who got killed in battle went to feast and fight with the gods for ever in Valholl (or Valhalla).

The mystery of the hungry bride (or Thor and his hammer)

One day, Thor woke up and looked around. 'Where's my hammer?' he roared. 'Who has stolen Mjollnir?'

'Well, I haven't got it,' said Loki. 'Not this time, anyway. Let's go and ask Freya for her feathered cloak, and then we can go looking for the thief.' Freya's cloak was made of feathers, and if you wore it you could fly.

'Of course you can borrow it,' said Freya. 'I would lend it even if it were made of gold.' Using the cloak, Loki flew to Giantland and asked Thrym, King of the Giants, if he knew anything about a missing hammer.

Thrym laughed. 'Yes, I've hidden it forty miles underground and you can't have it back until I get to marry Freya.'

'OK,' said Loki. 'I'll go and ask her.' So he went back to Freya.

'You have GOT to be kidding,' said Freya. 'Have you *seen* Thrym? I mean, like, totally gross!'

'But if we don't get back Mjollnir, the Giants will kill us!' said Loki. 'We *really* need that hammer!'

'And I *really* don't want to go to Giantland,' she protested.

'Well, all right,' said Loki. 'I have a plan, actually. All I need is some pretty clothes. Thor, you may not like this, but . . .'

THE WEDDING FEAST BEGINS

So the wedding was arranged. Loki flew back to Giantland, with a beautiful blushing bride. Admittedly, the bride did seem to have a bit of a facial hair problem, and more muscles than was usual for goddesses. But Thrym (who was short-sighted) had a look, and what he could see under the veil looked fine to him.

The wedding feast was prepared, and all the Giants began to eat. But no one ate more than the bride, who devoured a whole ox and eight salmon. And that was just the entree.

'She eats a lot,' said Thrym admiringly.

'Freya didn't eat for eight days and nights, so eager was she to come to Giantland,' Loki explained.

Thrym lifted up the bride's veil to kiss her, and staggered back against the wall. 'Why are Freya's eyes so fiery?' he asked.

'She didn't sleep for eight days and nights, so eager was she to come to Giantland,' said Loki.

'All right,' said Thrym. 'Bring out Thor's hammer.' (You needed a hammer to solemnise a Viking marriage.)

As soon as Mjollnir was brought out, the blushing bride laughed, grabbed it and killed Thrym, together with lots of other Giants. Then Thor and Loki went back to Asgarth.

The Giants were certainly strong and dangerous, but they could lose a battle of wits with a cheese sandwich.

The doom of the gods

The sad thing was that the gods knew they were doomed. In a long poem called *Voluspa*, Othin goes to ask a sibyl (a wise woman) about the end of the world. She tells him that eventually the Giants will destroy the gods.

She keeps telling Othin more and worse things. Every so often she asks, 'Would you know more?', meaning 'Do you want me to go on?'

Othin says yes, he has to hear it all. He learns that Loki (who is the son of a Giant) will join the Giants, sailing in a ship made from the toenails of dead men. The terrible wolf Garm has been held on a long chain since the beginning of time. He will break the chain and swallow the sun and moon. Mithgarthsorm (the great serpent who winds around the world) will also break free.

'Would you know more?' she asks again.

'Yes, go on,' says Othin. 'I'm listening.'

The sibyl says (or sings),

How fare the gods? How fare the Elves?
All Giantland trembles; the Gods meet,
the dwarves groan at their stone doors
guiding the rock-wall. Well? Would you know more?

Garm howls before Jutting Cave:
the rope will snap and the wolf run free.
I know much history, and I see further:
the terrible doom of the gods in battle.

Frost drives westward raising his shield aloft;
Earth-Serpent twists in Giant-mood.
The Dragon beats the waves, the eagle screams,
yellow-beaked rends the dead. Nail-Ship breaks loose.

This was the ship made from the toenails of dead men. The poem goes on, telling us who sailed on the ship and the battles they fought. It's chaos.

Rocks crash, trolls topple, roof-beams tumble
down to hell, and the heavens split . . .

And later, the whole world is destroyed.

The sun blackens, earth sinks in the sea
bright stars turn out of the sky.
Smoke and fire rage, flames lick
around the feet of highest heaven.
Reek and steam broil the air;
flame tongues lick against heaven itself.

Because the Vikings believed that their world would fall into ruin, they thought the only thing really worth having was fame after you were dead. It made them unbelievably brave and steadfast, but it wasn't a very comfortable religion. No wonder Njal said about the coming of Christianity, 'In my view the new faith is much better. Happy the man who accepts it.'

'Let's all be Christians together – or else!'

The Vikings had their own way of handling the new religion with its hero Jesus Christ. About 1000 years ago, King Olaf Tryggvason of Norway decided that he was a Christian, and everybody else must be too. Or else. The missionary he sent to Iceland was called Thangbrand. Thangbrand had a very short way with people who didn't agree with him. A man named Thorkel challenged him to a duel. Thangbrand used a crucifix instead of a shield in his left hand, but in his right hand he had a regular steel sword, which he used to kill Thorkel.

The Icelanders must have been impressed. They eventually decided at the Althing that the new religion was better, and so they all became Christians.

GODLY DAYS

Othin, Thor and all the rest of the gods were finished. Or were they? Some Icelanders still believe in their old gods. And they are remembered in our names for days of the week.

Tuesday was Tyr's day
(Tyr was the son of Othin)

Wednesday was Woden's day
(Woden is the Old English spelling of Othin)

Thursday was Thor's day

Friday was Frigg's day
(Frigg was Othin's wife)

9

DEFEAT

For all their poetry and story-telling, the Vikings were still spending a lot of time causing headaches for everyone else. In the end, people got a bit fed up. King Alfred the Great of Wessex showed what you could do to stop them. He became king of Wessex when the Viking raids were at their fiercest, and nearly all the rest of England had been conquered. He fought nine battles against them in 870 CE, his first year as king.

When another huge Viking army turned up in 878, he was ready for them. He had ships of his own by now, and a ring of fortified towns all around his kingdom. In times of trouble, he had half his army working on their farms and the other half in the field ready to give battle. Every now and again the two halves would swap places. There was always an army in the field anywhere the Vikings landed. Meanwhile, the farms were still producing food, and soldiers got to see their families. It was a good system.

Finally Alfred won a decisive battle at Eddington and the Viking army was destroyed. 'I guess we *really* screwed up this time,' they thought. Guthrum (one of the leaders) asked if he could become a Christian, and would Alfred be his godfather? Since they would now be fellow-Christians,

Alfred agreed. He and Guthrum became friends and their armies never fought each other again.

Viking ships kept turning up, but Alfred's children Edward and Aethelflaed carried on the good work and won back a lot more land from the invaders.

Not at all nutty

By the year 1000, the Vikings were getting the upper hand in England again. In 1016, Knut the Great became king not only of Norway and Denmark, but of England as well. Knut was able to stop the Viking raids, because he also ruled the countries Vikings came from. Everyone lived in peace while he was on the throne.

Knut (or Canute) was the son of Svein Forkbeard, a Christian and a clever man. There's a famous story about him. His courtiers kept telling him how good he was. 'Sire, you are so powerful you could command the seas!' Knut was too sensible to go along with this rubbish. So he had his throne brought down to the edge of the sea. The tide was coming in, and Knut commanded the waves to retreat. In came the waves, and (naturally) Knut and the courtiers got very wet.

'See?' said Knut. 'The power of kings is empty. There is only one king worthy of honour, and that is God Himself.'

Time's up!

The times when you could go around stealing anything that wasn't nailed down were over. Ireland was the last to win peace. The Vikings had long used it as their own personal playground, but in 1014 the Christian king Brian Mac Kennedy fought and won a huge battle against them at Clontarf. The Vikings were utterly defeated.

A tale of two Harolds

There was still one Viking who wouldn't let go. By the year 1066, Harald the Ruthless was getting old. (He was 50, which was ancient for a Viking.) He had spent his whole life fighting, beating people up, stealing treasure and storming cities. He wasn't going to give up just when he'd got to be good at it. He decided that it would be a great idea to become King of England. He landed with an enormous army of Vikings and took over the city of York.

'Well, you can't be King of England because the last time I looked, I was,' said Harold Godwinsson.

(Harold was a pretty popular name in the eleventh century.)

Harald the Ruthless then decided to bargain. His messenger Tostig asked, 'What will you offer to King Harald?'

'Seven feet of earth, or maybe more. He is bigger than other men,' was the answer. So the battle began, Harald was killed and the Viking army destroyed. Harald the Ruthless had gone Viking once too often. And after that, his countrymen took the hint. They weren't going to be allowed to get away with this stuff any more.

The last of the Viking conquerors

The bad news for the surviving King Harold (Godwinsson) is that another army of Vikings under William the Bastard was setting out from Normandy, France.[7] Harold was killed and William took over England. He's been called William the Conqueror ever since.

The Viking Age was over. Or was it? Read on . . .

[7] Well, ex-Vikings. The Normans had originally been Vikings, but had settled down in France over 100 years before.

10

VIKING REPLAY

Imagine a whole lot of old people running around in costumes waving swords and acting out battles that happened 1000 years ago. It may sound ridiculous, but it happens. Who are these people, and why do they do it?

The New Varangian Guard

The original Varangian Guard was the Emperor's Viking bodyguard in Constantinople – a top unit of soldiers 1000 years ago. The New Varangian Guard (NVG) is a bunch of people who copy these soldiers. Members dress up in Viking (or Byzantine) clothes, play Viking games, camp in Viking tents, eat Viking food and fight Viking battles with real Viking armour and weapons.

The NVG started in Australia, and now has groups in many parts of the country. It also has branches in the USA, the UK and Italy. They believe that proper medieval fighting means metal weapons. It looks fantastic, but it's a bit hair-raising when a steel sword slices past your nose!

The Society for Creative Anachronisms

The Society for Creative Anachronisms (SCA) is a world-wide organisation which aims to re-create the Middle Ages (pre-1600). Members can choose any character they like, and many have chosen to be Vikings. SCA festivals can be big affairs, with up to

800 people camping in a variety of medieval tents and pavilions and living the medieval life. They also fight tournaments and full-scale wars.

SCA fighting is rather different from NVG fighting. Fighters use wooden swords just as medieval knights did when they were practising. This means you can hit your opponent quite hard, which you can't do if you have a real sword or axe. A steel sword, properly used, would probably slice through even metal armour. The SCA thinks that real weapons are too scary to use on the battlefield.

Of course, all these groups have strict safety rules for combat. They don't want anybody to get injured.

The SCA has hundreds of branches in many countries. Most are in the USA, but there's one called the Kingdom of Lochac which covers Australia and New Zealand.

Why spend your weekends (and often weeknights as well) dressing up in ancient costumes? The short answer is that it's fun. More than that, it's a kind of magic. After a while it gets you in, and you can't imagine life without it.

Go Vikings!

It's not surprising that so many people admire the Viking way of life. Some admire the Norse people for their courage and blood-chilling ferocity in battle. Others admire their beautiful longships. Certain Viking ideas seem very modern – like the belief that women aren't owned by their fathers and husbands. Or the idea that 'Just because you're king doesn't mean I should bow down to you!' The way they governed, with the laws made in an assembly, fits well with our ideals of democracy. (The English word 'law' is really a Viking word.) The Vikings were adventurers and leaders, people full of spirit. We can all admire that.

QUIZ

(Note: You may need to tick more than one answer for each question. There are 21 correct answers. See if you can get them all.)

1 The word 'Viking' means:

(a) a Scandinavian warrior ☐ (b) a hatchback sedan ☐
(c) a kind of bushwalking ☐ (d) sailing into people's countries and stealing things ☐

2 Vikings lived in:

(a) Sweden ☐ (b) Greenland ☐
(c) Antarctica ☐ (d) Hollywood ☐

3 The Vikings traded in:

(a) furs and skins ☐ (b) jewellery ☐
(c) iPods ☐ (d) slaves ☐

4 If captured by a Viking you should say:

(a) 'This looks like a fairly bad day for me.' ☐
(b) 'Hey, fishbreath!' ☐ (c) 'My battle-axe is called Sam.' ☐
(d) 'There's a big abbey with lots of gold over there.' ☐

5 Viking houses were made of:

(a) dead men's bones ☐ (b) stone ☐
(c) turf ☐ (d) gingerbread ☐

6 You are invited to a Viking dinner. You can expect to eat:

(a) pizza and cheese ☐ (b) roast reindeer ☐
(c) whale steaks ☐ (d) KFC ☐

7 Vikings went by sea to:

(a) America ☐ (b) Australia ☐
(c) Antarctica ☐ (d) Africa ☐

8 Next to the skin, the Vikings wore:

(a) nothing ☐ (b) leather ☐ (c) linen ☐
(d) Bonds Cottontails ☐

9 Which of these aren't real Viking names?

(a) Ulf the Unwashed ☐ (b) Gunnar Sheepsson ☐
(c) Eystein Fart ☐ (d) Bruce the Strange ☐

10 Vikings usually won battles because they:

(a) really wanted to ☐ (b) had better weapons ☐
(c) ate weird mushrooms ☐ (d) had spent a really boring week on a smelly boat and weren't going home without a showbag ☐

ANSWERS: **1** a,d **2** a,b **3** a,b,d **4** a,d
5 b,c **6** a,b,c **7** a,d **8** c **9** b,d **10** b,d

DAVID GREAGG first got interested in the Vikings when he learnt to speak Old Norse at university. He later went to Iceland where he walked on glaciers, climbed up active volcanoes and went swimming in the Arctic Ocean, just for the hell of it. In the Society for Creative Anachronisms he is known as Baron Master Dafydd of the Glens and fights for Lord Rioghan's Bearded Axemen. He is also an accredited wizard. You can find his website at: www.geocities.com/wizard_foots

BINNY HOBBS has been drawing ever since she could hold a pencil. At school she drew or doodled on anything that kept still. She thought she'd be an architect, but she couldn't stand all the straight lines. Now she draws for clients all around the globe: raccoons for Japan, pigs for Hawaii, ducks and cowboys for the USA. Her characters live on TV, in magazines, books, CDs and on Bond's children's clothes.

hi!

Binny lives in Sydney with her husband Alex and faithful helper Charlie the border collie. Her website is at: www.binny.com.au

THANKS

Thanks to Margaret Birtley for teaching me Old Norse, Bernard Muir for teaching me Anglo-Saxon, Saarlands/Axemen for being great comrades in arms, House Attica for inspiration, and Kerry Greenwood for support, patience, advice and everything else.

David Greagg

The publishers would like to thank Dr Timothy Dawson for fact-checking. Thanks to Jomsvikings (www.jomsvikings.com) for the photographs on pages viii, 2, 37, 73, 76, 77 and 81, and Iarl Sir Alfar of Attica for the photograph on page 79. Thanks also to istockphoto.com and the photographers named for images appearing on the following pages: Jan Bily (parchment used throughout text); page 15 Fredrik Wall (Viking home in Stockholm); page 22 Jacob Jensen (Danish Viking longship); page 29 Dirk Paessler (icebergs in Jokulsarlon Glacier Lake, Iceland); page 59 duckycards (stone tablet); page 60 Johnny Magnusson (rune stone in Sweden).

TIMELINE

Note: 'CE' stands for 'Common Era'. It is based on the Christian calendar, so 400 CE is 400 years after Christ's birth.

400 CE Vikings find Sweden boring because Volvo car not invented yet. They move to Denmark and Norway.

410–550 Fall of Roman Empire. Vikings couldn't care less.

793 Viking tourists destroy Lindisfarne because there was nothing to do on Sunday.

795 The Irish start telling Viking jokes. Vikings attack Ireland.

865 Even though they have been warned about the weather, Vikings settle in England and invent the cheese sandwich.

870 Alfred takes over Wessex.

878 Battle of Eddington.
Alfred 1, Vikings 0.

880 Vikings set out for Constantinople, get lost and capture Kiev instead by mistake. Harald of Norway stops washing his hair.

890 Harald washes hair.
Day of rejoicing proclaimed by Norwegian hairdressers.

892 More Viking tourists invade England on cheap package deal. No hot water; hotels haven't been built yet. Vikings defeated.

930 Vikings settle in Iceland and invent spa-bath.

982 Erik the Red settles in Greenland, which wasn't.

986 Bjarni Herjolfson goes looking for Greenland and finds Canada.

1000 Olaf Tryggvason gets religion: Vikings convert to Christianity.

Leif Eriksson settles in America, fails to invent hamburger.

1014 Vikings refuse to pay rent to Irish or return lawn-mower.

Battle of Clontarf: Irish 1, Vikings 0.

1016 Knut the Great of Norway and Denmark suddenly Knut of England as well. English relieved. Knut gets wet.

1066 Harald the Ruthless makes takeover bid for England. English unimpressed, Vikings destroyed.

William the Bastard wins Battle of Hastings. Later called William the Conqueror, or just Yessir.

End of Viking Age

WHERE TO FIND OUT MORE

Websites

- www.vikinglady.com
- www.viking.no/
- www.bbc.co.uk/history (follow prompts to Vikings)
- www.smplanet.com/kids/history.html

For Viking cookery, go to

- http://viking.no./e/life/food/e-flatbr.html
  (this is the Viking pizza source)

The website of the New Varangian Guard is at

- http://nvg.org.au

The website of the Society for Creative Anachronisms is at

- http://www.sca.org.au

Other re-enactment groups in Australia are listed at

- www.arlho.net

Books

FICTION

Anna Ciddor, Viking Magic trilogy: *Runestone*, *Wolfspell* and *Stormriders*, Allen & Unwin, Sydney, 2002, 2003, 2004

For teachers

Magnus Magnusson, *Vikings!*, The Bodley Head, London, 1980

E.V. Gordon, *An Introduction to Old Norse*, Clarendon Press, Oxford, 1927

Njal's Saga, translated by M. Magnusson & H. Palsson, Penguin, Harmondsworth, 1960

Hrafnkel's Saga & Other Stories, translated by H. Palsson, Penguin, Harmondsworth, 1971

INDEX